The Greater One

A Testament to the Faithfulness of God

By: Dawn Thomas

Edited by Sheila Harper

Acknowledgement

I would like to express my sincerest appreciation for Sheila Harper who undertook the painstaking task of editing this book for me. I cannot truly express the gratitude that I have for that labor of love. I am forever thankful for your love, friendship, and the blessing you have been in my life!

Table of Contents

Foreword

I've been encouraged to write a book many times by various people who know me and are aware of the struggles, trials, temptations, heartaches and failures I have encountered. Yet I always come out on the other side with a clear and concise knowledge that "The Greater One" is definitely living in me and He is GREATER than he who lives in the world. My desire is not necessarily to "tell my story" but rather to tell of the great and marvelous grace and mercies of my Lord and Savior Jesus Christ who has never failed me. I will tell you, I have been married three times. I have three children, twin sons aged 33 and a daughter age 24 as well as a grandson who is seven years old. That being said, the follow pages will include many scriptures, sprinkled with what I pray are God-inspired words of wisdom. I hope you enjoy the personal experiences I have shared for the purpose of illustrating God's love, grace, and mercies.

1 John 4:4 (NLT)

4 But you belong to God, my dear children. You have already won a victory over those people, because the Spirit who lives in you is greater than the spirit who lives in the world.

It is my prayer that God will use this book to touch as many lives and hearts as possible for His glory and honor. I believe He will bring a new revelation of His goodness, mercies, grace, and faithfulness thereby, giving hope to the hopeless. In doing so, I pray this book also touches the hearts of the lost to know God in a way they never have before.

God, I ask that You bless the work of my hands right now and cause the words You have for the audience reading this book to be spilled out on the following pages. Get me and my ego out of the way and let Your work and Your word be glorified.

Thank You Father for each person reading Your message in these pages right now. Bless

them and give them eyes to see, and ears to hear, what the Spirit would say to them. Open their hearts and minds to receive that which You have for them in the mighty name of Jesus. Amen and so be it.

Chapter 1
Fearfully and Wonderfully Made

Did you know that there is no such thing as "unplanned" when it comes to creation? God has plans for every single one of us. He told Adam and Eve to "be fruitful and multiply." He didn't say be careful and make sure you don't procreate at the wrong time. He certainly didn't say, if you mess up and get pregnant when you weren't planning for it then kill the baby.

The psalmist David said, *I praise you because I am fearfully and wonderfully made; your works are wonderful, I know that full well. Psalm 139:14 (NIV)*

God created every intricate detail of our being in the image of Himself. He has a plan and a purpose for everything He has created. It is not up to us to decide what that is. He gives us free will, but it doesn't change His plan for our lives, and He will take us from point A to point B the easiest way we will go.

Ephesians 2:10 (NIV)
For we are God's handiwork, created in Christ Jesus to do good works, which God prepared in advance for us to do.

As we see in Ephesians, we are God's handiwork. He created us to do good works that He already has planned in advance for us to do! I get excited when I think about God's plans for me and all He has yet for me to do. I claim that verse over my life and the lives of my children and grandson almost daily. I thank Him that He will fulfill His perfect plan and purpose in my life and in the lives of my children.

Psalm 139:13 (NIV)
For you created my inmost being; you knit me together in my mother's womb.

Jeremiah 1:5 (NIV)

"Before I formed you in the womb I knew you, before you were born I set you apart

The scriptures tell us we are fearfully and wonderfully made and that God created our "inmost being" when He knit us together in our mother's womb. Before He formed us in that womb, He already knew us! I want you to know right this moment that whoever you are, God had a purpose for you before anyone had an opinion. You are no accident and you weren't "unplanned." You arrived on this planet exactly when God intended you to arrive. There are no accidents and there's no such thing as "unplanned," not in God's Kingdom.

Father I ask that you touch the hearts and minds of those reading this chapter and heal what needs healing. Let them know that they are loved with an everlasting love that never fails and never changes. Give them peace in knowing their worth and value in You, the Creator who knew them before they were ever formed in the womb.

Chapter 2
Amazing Grace

I am so thankful for a loving, merciful, forgiving Father God. I make it a point to thank Him daily for all He has done for me. I've learned to be grateful for the good times and the not so good times in my life. I've come to understand, He uses them all for my good and His most loving outcome. I'm sure that theme will be repeated often throughout this text. After all, repetition is how we learn and how it gets into our spirit to become a deeply imbedded belief.

I know He is loving, merciful, forgiving and kind because I have experienced all of that from Him firsthand. I told you in the Foreword that I've been married three times. I was 18 the first time I got married. I had gotten pregnant and felt that getting married was "the right thing to do." We had planned to be married anyway, just not as quickly as we did. We eloped on October 18, 1986 on our way to visit his parents in Kentucky. When we returned home from that trip I walked into my parent's house and my mother was sitting in the living room on the phone. She took one look at me and asked, "What have you done?" I stretched out my arm and showed her my wedding band. I'm pretty sure I rendered her speechless at that moment. I didn't tell her I was pregnant, and she didn't ask.

A few months into my pregnancy I was diagnosed with mild dysplasia. I had no idea what that was, but my doctor did not really seem concerned, so I wasn't either. However, my mother apparently spoke to one of her friends who was a nurse, about my condition. This friend informed her mild dysplasia was the beginning stage of cervical cancer. My mother called my doctor's office to inquire about the condition. At that point in time as far as my mother knew, my due date was mid-July. The person she spoke with at the doctor's office said "Well let's see, her due date is June 1st, so....." Later that afternoon my mother conveyed the conversation to me to let me know she now knew the reason we had eloped. She told me she hoped that wasn't the only reason I got married.

A little later in my pregnancy I was diagnosed with gestational diabetes. I was sent to see a nutritionist who explained to me foods I should and shouldn't be eating in order for the baby to have optimal health during gestation. At that time I had no idea I was carrying twins and neither did my doctor. However, I was sick every single day vomiting throughout each day from the time my feet hit the floor until my head hit the pillow. Because of my extreme morning sickness, I told my husband that if he wanted more than one child he better be praying for twins. It turns out twins double everything including "morning sickness."

Five weeks before my due date I started having Braxton Hicks contractions. My doctor sent me to the hospital to be checked and monitored. She then sent me for an ultrasound to see if the baby's head was still in position. I had been given medication to stop the Braxton Hicks contractions and was therefore a bit "drunk." As the ultrasound tech was running the probe over my distended abdomen she seemed to be acting a little funny. She couldn't tell us anything about what she was seeing on the screen because she had to wait for the Radiologist to come in to tell us. When the Radiologist arrived, he looked at the screen with a puzzled expression. Now I was beginning to wonder what was wrong with my baby. He looked at me and then at my husband and said, "Well, I have some news for you." At this point I was a little scared but still a little loopy. He then asked, "What do you think about twins?" Our jaws dropped! I couldn't believe what I had just heard, but it definitely sobered me up immediately. My mother was waiting in my room on the 4th floor and somehow managed to hear the news before they wheeled me back.

Two weeks later I gave birth to two beautiful baby boys. One weighing 6 lbs. 10 oz., the other weighing 6 lbs. 3 oz. My doctor was as surprised as we were that there were two instead of one. She said that I hadn't mentioned any extra movement. I laughed and told her, "I'm 19 years old and this is my first pregnancy.... I didn't realize it was extra movement." I thought I was pregnant with an extra-large baby that liked to move a lot.

I learned many things about my husband after we married, that would have prevented me from marrying him at all had I not gotten pregnant. However, I don't know where I might be in life without my sons whom I love with every fiber of my being. That alone for me confirms God's word in *Romans 8:28* which says *"And we know that God causes everything to work together for the good of those who love God and are called according to his purpose for them."* (NLT). In spite of poor choices and decisions, God gave me two beautiful baby boys that I had the honor and privilege of raising. They have been a source of continuous joy and blessings for over 33 years now.

After being married to my first husband for five years, we divorced for a variety of reasons. Soon after, I started dating my second husband and we were married about eight months after we started dating. He is the father of my daughter. We were married for 17 years.

After we had been married for about six years, my husband took a job working nights and I only saw him on the weekends. His new job took so much of his time and energy I eventually succumbed to temptation and had an affair. I won't go into how or why that happened in this text because I don't want to make excuses for my bad decisions. After my husband learned of the affair, he still wanted to try to make the marriage work. At first, I had no desire to do so, but at some point, I felt as though it was what God would have me do. I ended up staying in that marriage for another 11 years. During that time I also made a determination to be the best, most Godly wife and mother I could be. I started attending church twice on Sundays and on Wednesday evenings as well. My husband however, did not have that same commitment. He may have gone to church with us a total of 7-10 times throughout the course of the next 11 years.

I endeavored to be the Godliest mother I could be. My sons probably still resent that to this day because they could never understand why they had to go to church if their step-father didn't. I would explain to them, they could make that decision once they were adults like he was but until then they would be going to church with me. I enjoyed going to church and became involved first in the choir and later in the youth ministry. I must say I was a bit disillusioned by it all and didn't realize for many years that church is a business like anything else. After attending the same church for 10 years, I was introduced to the book, "The Shack." In that book I learned the life of a Christian is about a relationship with our Lord and Savior Jesus Christ, not about religion and rituals. This book changed my life for the better. It helped me have a clearer understanding of what relationship with the Father, Son, and Holy Spirit really looks like. Because of that revelation knowledge I came to realize the earth would not stop moving on its axis if I missed a church service to be with family who were visiting from out of town, or for any reason really.

"The Church," is all of us who believe and profess that Jesus Christ is King of Kings and Lord of Lords and He is the one and only son of God who died for the sins of the entire world. That is the bottom line. We are to be His hands and feet and go out into the world to preach the gospel of the good news that Jesus has paid the price for all. With that being said, I came to a stunning realization I did not agree with the way my church at that time "did business." So, I started attending a different church that I believed was more in line with my newfound beliefs. The bible states in *Romans 8:1-2 (NIV) Therefore, there is now no condemnation for those who are in Christ Jesus, [2]because through Christ Jesus the law of the Spirit who gives life has set you free from the law of sin and death.*

Jesus paid the price one time for all sins that have ever been committed or ever will be committed. I felt as though the church I had been attending condemned everyone who didn't follow lock step with what they taught. No Bible that I have read says you have to be in church every time the doors are open. The one I read says we are the

Church and we are to go into all the world and share the gospel. Yes, it also says not to forsake fellowship one with another as some are in the habit of doing. But again, that is a far cry from legalistic, ritualistic church attendance.

At least 10 of the last 11 years of my second marriage were spent living basically as roommates. At that point I couldn't take it any longer. I had spent countless hours praying for my husband, for our marriage, for our family to what seemed like no avail and I finally gave up. I don't know whether he would have ever eventually come around or not. What I do know is that God gives each of us free will and that while my husband had not physically left the marriage, he had emotionally left it years before. I no longer felt that I was biblically bound to stay with him according to *1 Corinthians 7:15* which says *"However, if the one who is not a believer wishes to leave the Christian partner, let it be so. In such cases the Christian partner, whether husband or wife, is free to act. God has called you to live in peace,"* and so I filed for divorce.

I was spent both emotionally and mentally from the lack of love and affection. I believe that everyone has their limits and I had more than reached mine, for the second time in our marriage. I never strayed again, but I was accused of it, because the reality was, he never really forgave me, nor did he ever let me forget my transgression.

I was still drained mentally and emotionally when I encountered an old boyfriend from my teen years who seemed to be my knight in shining armor. We started seeing each other before the divorce was final and continued to date on and off for three and a half years. It was a toxic and tumultuous roller coaster of a relationship. In the beginning I did not realize the depth of his mental instability and emotional issues. He had lost his wife in a tragic boating accident the year before. He was also in the boat with her. He seemed so excited to see me and spend time with me I thought his feelings were genuine. I felt he had dealt with the loss of his wife. Now, I had never lost anyone close to me, so I had no idea what was going on under the surface. The reality is, he was not ready for another relationship. He hadn't appropriately dealt with the loss of his wife and couldn't cope with much in life because he constantly lived in the past. He had triggers that made him behave badly, push me away, push his son away etc. These episodes were fairly regular every month and I pretty much knew when to expect them. I'd "hold my breath" hoping that things would somehow be different and get better, but they didn't. It was like he didn't know how to just "be content."

After riding that roller coaster with him for 3 ½ years we married in January of 2013. I can't really say why I accepted his proposal. My inner man knew it was a bad idea. However, when things were "good" between us they were exceptionally good. I suppose I hoped that they could finally be exceptionally good all the time. Unfortunately, in May of 2013 I came home from work one evening for him to inform me that he didn't want to be married after all. We never argued per se, so I asked him what grounds he was going to file for divorce under. He informed me that I couldn't stop him from getting a divorce, nobody could. So, I proceeded to pack my things to leave. As I was packing, he paced back and forth in the living room like a caged lion. I apologized for taking so long as I had made the mistake of thinking it was my home. One month later, he begged me not to go through with the divorce that he had filed for. I knew I shouldn't have married him; however, I had convinced myself that he wouldn't have married me if he wasn't ready. By that point I was so mentally distraught from the years of being pushed away then pulled back that I believe it literally took marriage and divorce for me to finally let go of any hope of a relationship with him working out. I came to the realization the rest of my life would be a sick, twisted roller coaster of a ride if I had stayed with him. By the grace of God it finally ended with our divorce in November 2013.

I won't go into further detail about those parts of my life and story because I in no way want to give the devil any kind of glory for the destruction that he has caused in my life. I do however, want to give glory to God my Father for His amazing grace in seeing me through the darkest times of life. I want every person reading this to know your hope is in Christ. The God I serve is the God of "so much more." He is able to do so much more than we could ever possibly ask, think, or imagine, in and through our lives. You need only to believe.

My grandson was born in July 2012 and he brought so much joy and happiness to my life during a time that was wrought with darkness. God knows exactly what we need and exactly when we need it. God's grace is sufficient, and I am so thankful for that. I'm positive without him in my life at that time I would be in a much different place today.

Following my third divorce I spent several years doing what I wanted to, when I wanted to, and with whom I wanted. Now almost two years after my last relationship ended, I am happier and more peaceful and content than I probably have ever been in my life. I still believe God created me to be the wife of a Godly man, and over the last 18 months he has been training me to be still in the waiting. I believe I will receive every good and perfect gift God has for me, including that Godly husband. He created us for relationship and to be helpmates. I pray for my future husband daily and trust that God is preparing his heart and mind to receive me as his wife just as He is preparing me to receive him as my husband. I believe I needed to get to a place of truly being the person my future husband is looking for. Eighteen months ago, I knew I wouldn't be attractive to the kind of person I want to marry. It is only by God's amazing grace that I gained revelation knowledge in the middle of my brokenness. If He had not imparted that wisdom to me, I'm afraid to consider the path of self-destruction I might have taken.

Chapter 3
Don't Lose Faith

I'm not sure how many of you realize it, but the devil knows you...he studies you like a book. While God's plan is to do you good and not harm, to give you hope and a future, the devil's plan is to destroy you any way he can. It is his goal to make you doubt God. It is the devil's goal to make you question God's sovereignty, His promises, and His faithfulness. I get extremely frustrated when I see him winning that battle of the mind with believers who know better. Yet I know the devil knows us and knows how to hit below the belt by making us question our faith and trust in the Lord. I also know God is still faithful to fulfill His promises. When you encounter someone whose faith is waning, try not to get too frustrated with them (and I'm preaching to the choir here, because it's very difficult for me not to get frustrated myself). I've had the privilege of loving some of my friends enough to speak the truth of the Word of God in love to them being fully aware they already knew the Word I was speaking. When those you love lose sight of God's truth you must love them through the immediate situation that they're going through and continue to lift them up in prayer covering them with the blood of Jesus. It is our responsibility as fellow believers in the Lord to lift and hold each other up when we encounter someone who has not the strength to lift themselves.

Be persistent in your faith and prayer. God tells us to ask and keep on asking and it will be done. Don't ask once then give up because you don't see immediate results, or God doesn't work it out the way you think it should be worked out. He wants to give us good things and do good things in our lives. Hold on to His promises because He is faithful to perform them.

I know how easy it is to become discouraged and despondent when you don't see God working in your life, the lives of your family members, your situation etc. That's exactly what the devil wants. He wants you to give up on God, to give up on seeing Him work and move in your life. *John 5:17* says, *"But Jesus replied, 'My Father is always working, and so am I.'"* We must never lose sight of the fact that Jesus is always working on our behalf, even when we don't see it or feel it. We are admonished to live by "faith" not by "sight." How many of do that when the going gets tough? It's hard to stay focused on how big our God is when all you can think about is how big your problems are. Our battles are not of flesh and blood so I encourage you don't give up...whatever your need is today, don't give up and don't give in. Start agreeing with the word of God that He is able to do so much more than you can ask, think or possibly imagine by His power at work in YOU! Transform your mind by renewing it in the Word of God.

Hebrews 11:6-8 (NIV)
6And without faith it is impossible to please God, because anyone who comes to him must believe that He exists and that He rewards those who earnestly seek him.
7By faith Noah, when warned about things not yet seen, in holy fear built an ark to save his family. By

his faith he condemned the world and became heir of the righteousness that is in keeping with faith. [8]By faith Abraham, when called to go to a place he would later receive as his inheritance, obeyed and went, even though he did not know where he was going.

Chapter 4
God's Promises

My journey has been one of learning to trust and rest in God's promises. What an amazing journey it has been. My daughter and I have grown closer to each other than we have ever been, and closer to our heavenly Father in the process. I have been extremely blessed by God's amazing grace.

My daughter and I spent three months going through Max Lucado's Bible Study "Unshakable Hope." This book explains God's promises in detail. Throughout the course of the three months we met together to study the book and the Bible we grew closer to each other and we saw many prayers answered.

One of the things we learned in our journey is the fact that we are created in the image of God is a promise. *Genesis 1:3, 4, 6, 9, 11, 14, 20, 24, and 26* begin with *"and God said"* as He created the entire universe and everything in it with the spoken word. *Genesis 1:27* says He created us in His image. If we're created in His image then our words must also hold tremendous power. But even more powerful than that is when we speak His word into our lives and the lives of others. I also believe, when you pray the Word you're praying His will. I try to use as much scripture as possible when praying for and with people so that I'm speaking His will over their lives as we agree together in prayer.

Proverbs 18:21 also speaks of the power of the tongue. Life and Death are extremely powerful. We can speak life into a situation, circumstance, or life of another or we can speak death to the same. I believe when you speak the word of God, and give voice to His promises you're speaking life and His will. One of the promises that I cling to for my family is in **Joshua 24:15** – *as for me and my family, we will serve the Lord.* I believe claiming God's promises out loud, where our ears can hear, sets His spiritual forces into motion on our behalf.

I know many people, including myself, often wonder why some prayers are answered and others are not. However, on the other hand I also believe that all prayers are answered, the answer just may not be the answer we seek. Some things we will never comprehend this side of heaven. We are not meant to know or understand everything though. Our finite minds cannot begin to comprehend an infinite God. As we trust Him, we learn that He will take what the devil means for evil and turn it for our good and His most loving outcome.

God's sovereign plan is not for us to judge. That being said, I would like to point out that God asks us what we want Him to do (Matthew 10:51) and often we do not pray specifically. He tells us to bring everything, every prayer and petition to Him with thanksgiving (as though it has already been done) and He will give us peace that transcends all natural reasoning or understanding. I think we often claim whatever our problem or issue may be as our own, holding it closely to us instead of releasing it to the Lord. We can cast all of our cares on Him for He cares for us. Then we keep our thoughts fixed and focused on the problem instead of keeping them fixed and focused on the One who asks, "What do you want Me to do for you?"

When He tells us to bring our prayers and petitions to Him with thanksgiving, it doesn't just mean thanking Him for what He's already done. We can thank Him in advance for what He's going to do that we haven't yet seen manifest in the natural physical realm.

I'd like to point out that God told Abram to start calling himself Abraham (Father of many nations) well before he received the son God had promised him...and Abraham did it! Names had significant meaning in that era, so don't you know that his family, friends, and business associates thought he was crazy for calling himself Abraham? After all, both he and Sarah were well past their "child-bearing" years. That's what I mean by thank Him for your prayer already being answered. Words are powerful. God created the whole universe with His spoken word...we have the same power when we speak His word.

His word says nothing is impossible with Him; nothing is too difficult for Him. According to *Jerimiah 29:11*, He has a plan and purpose for your life and His plan is to do you good and not harm, to give you hope and a future. His word says that surely there is a future and your hope will not be cut off *(Proverbs 23:18)*. His word says that He is able to do far over and exceedingly above all that you ask, think or even dare to imagine *(Ephesians 3:20)*. His word says if He is for you, then no foe can stand against you *(Romans 8:31)*. His word says the same Spirit that raised Christ from the dead dwells in me *(Romans 8:11)*.

When the devil starts trying to tell me his lies, I like to tell Him what my God has to say about them. So instead of telling my All Mighty God how big my problems are, I start telling my problems how BIG and STRONG and MIGHTY my GOD is!

God's promises are received through faith, not through any actions or performances of our own. *Romans 4:13-15 (NLT) states, "Clearly, God's promise to give the whole earth to Abraham and his descendants was based not on his obedience to God's law, but on a right relationship with God that comes by faith. 14If God's promise is only for those* *who obey the law, then faith is not necessary and the promise is pointless. ¹⁵For the law always brings punishment on those who try to obey it. (The only way to avoid breaking the law is to have no law to break!)"*

God sent his son Emmanuel to be with us always. He will never leave us or forsake us. He has sent his Holy Spirit to be our Helper. He is the same yesterday, today and forever. These are all promises of God. We can stand firmly on His word and believe what it says is true. God is truth and love and light.

Matthew 7:8 For everyone who asks will receive, and anyone who seeks will find, and the door will be opened to those who knock. All we have to do is ask! The Bible also says we have not because we ask not.... So, we are to ask and keep on asking according to *Matthew 7:7 (AMP).*

God promises to give us good things. *Matthew 7:11 (NLT)* states, *"So if you sinful people know how to give good gifts to your children, how much more will your heavenly Father give good gifts to those who ask him."* What have you asked God for in faith believing it will be done?

The reality is, we cannot perform perfectly enough to ever earn our way into heaven, or being sons and daughters of God. We only attain entrance to heaven and relationship with the Father through faith in God's grace/unmerited favor which is His ultimate promise to us.

After completing the Bible study my daughter, she and I decided we would continue with our Bible study, and ask other women we know to join us in our journey. I want everyone I know to get in on the goodness of God and all He has for us!

Chapter 5
Matters of the Heart

We only know another person as well as they want us to know them. Only God knows the human heart and has the right to judge. 1 Kings 8:39 (NLT) states, "then hear from heaven where you live, and forgive. Give your people what their actions deserve, for you alone know each human heart." We often presume to know others when we do not "know" them at all. It has amazed me throughout the course of my life how people who may know a little bit about me presume that because of that they actually "know" me.

I dare say everyone on the face of this earth has thoughts they keep tightly to themselves and to not dare say out loud to another human being. They may fear ridicule, rejection, loathing. At any rate we cannot really "know" anyone but ourselves. Therefore, it is presumptuous and dangerous to think we truly know anyone.

People often walk the fine line of judgement when they think they know someone else's heart.

It is best to not be presumptuous and rather to pray for your fellowman when you believe something is amiss. As Luke 6:37 says, "Do not judge others, and you will not be judged. Do not condemn others, or it will all come back against you. Forgive others, and you will be forgiven."

We know Satan is the accuser of the brethren, but sometimes we can be as well. You never know what someone is going through in their life. Their actions do not define who they are. If they have been saved they are a new creation in Christ. They are the Righteousness of God in Christ. They are your brothers and sisters in Christ. Whatever sin someone may be participating in at any given time does not define them. It is not our job to convict, it is our job to love. It is the Holy Spirit's job to convict. So if you want to walk in love, pray for the Holy Spirit to convict them of their Righteousness. Don't go around talking about their unrighteousness to others. *Father forgive me for any time that I have walked that line of judgement, and help me to walk in and convey your love instead.*

It's all about love…

Matthew 22:37 Jesus replied: "'Love the Lord your God with all your heart and with all your soul and with all your mind.' This is the first and greatest commandment. And the second is like it: 'Love your neighbor as yourself.' All the Law and the Prophets hang on these two commandments."

1 Corinthians 13:4-8, 13 ⁴Love is patient, love is kind. It does not envy, it does not boast, it is not proud. It does not dishonor others, it is not self-seeking, it is not easily angered, it keeps no record of wrongs. Love does not delight in evil but rejoices with the truth. It always protects, always, trusts, always hopes, always perseveres. Love never fails. But where there are prophecies, they will cease; where there are tongues, they will be stilled, where there is knowledge, it will pass away. ¹³And now these three remain: faith, hope and love. But the greatest of these is love.

John 3:16 For God so loved the world that he gave his one and only Son, that whoever believes in him shall not perish but have eternal life.

Think about that last verse for a moment. Do you have children of your own? If so, can you imagine giving any one of them to die on a cross to save someone else? I have three children, and I simply cannot fathom the sacrifice of our Father and His son Jesus Christ. Jesus knew what was going to happen before He ever came to this earth as a baby. He did it anyway. He did it for you, He did it for me, He did it for humanity! For God so loved the WORLD... that's all of us! But, if you were the only one here, Jesus still would have come and died on the cross to save you from your sins. I don't think He's asking too much when He asks us to walk in love toward our fellowman. Never let someone's behavior define who they are to you. They were created in the image of God, just like you were. And don't assume that you know someone, just because you know something about them.

Chapter 6
Shame

Often when we know we have walked outside the Father's will; the devil will try to convince us that we are not worthy of the Father's grace. The reality is God is not willing that any should perish. However, the shame of willful disobedience will cause us to separate ourselves from the Father as Adam and Eve did in the garden when they tried to hide from him because of their shame.

Genesis 3:6-8
⁶ The woman was convinced. She saw that the tree was beautiful, and its fruit looked delicious, and she wanted the wisdom it would give her. So, she took some of the fruit and ate it. Then she gave some to her husband, who was with her, and he ate it, too. ⁷ At that moment their eyes were opened, and they suddenly felt shame at their nakedness. So, they sewed fig leaves together to cover

themselves. [8] When the cool evening breezes were blowing, the man and his wife heard the Lord God walking about in the garden. So, they hid from the Lord God among the trees.

Romans 8:1 (AMP)
Therefore, there is now no condemnation [no guilty verdict, no punishment] for those who are in Christ Jesus [who believe in Him as personal Lord and Savior].

Do you know why Satan uses shame? He wants to destroy us. If he can convince us we are guilty and should be ashamed of our actions, then he can keep us from relationship with the Father. He is subtle about it too. He may not use an all-out straightforward attack, but rather nagging little thoughts he will insert here and there to make us feel shameful and unworthy.

As Christians, the moment we ask Jesus to forgive us there is no further condemnation because we are in Him! So, when the devil tries to remind you of what you have done you need to remind him of who your Savior is; He says, "Not guilty, I've already paid for that."

The reality is, we don't have to walk around with our heads hung low feeling guilty and ashamed of our pasts because Jesus died on the cross to pay the price for all of our transgressions. He doesn't accuse and condemn us so neither should we condemn ourselves or each other through the lies of the enemy.

Revelation 12:9-11 (NKJV)
9 So the great dragon was cast out, that serpent of old, called the Devil and Satan, who deceives the whole world; he was cast to the earth, and his angels were cast out with him. 10 Then I heard a loud voice saying in heaven, "Now salvation, and strength, and the kingdom of our God, and the power of His Christ have come, for the accuser of our brethren, who accused them before our God day and night, has been cast down. 11 And they overcame him by the blood of the Lamb and by the word of their testimony, and they did not love their lives to the death.

The word of God says that the devil or Satan is the accuser of the brethren, (that's you and me) and he accuses us before the throne of God day and night. It also says that we overcome the devil by the blood of the Lamb (Jesus Christ) and the word of our testimony. So again, when the devil starts trying to remind you of your past just remind him of the cleansing, atoning, saving blood of Jesus that already paid for it. And while you're at it, you can remind him of his destiny in the lake of fire.

Hebrews 12:1-2 (AMPC)
1 Therefore then, since we are surrounded by so great a cloud of witnesses [who have borne testimony to the Truth], let us strip off and throw aside every encumbrance (unnecessary weight) and that sin which so readily (deftly and cleverly) clings to and entangles us, and let us run with patient endurance and steady and active persistence the appointed course of the race that is set before us,
2 Looking away [from all that will distract] to Jesus, Who is the Leader and the Source of our faith

[giving the first incentive for our belief] and is also its Finisher [bringing it to maturity and perfection]. He, for the joy [of obtaining the prize] that was set before Him, endured the cross, despising and ignoring the shame, and is now seated at the right hand of the throne of God.

When the devil tries to get you distracted by making you feel guilty and ashamed remember the shame that Jesus bore on the cross. Tell the devil your shame it has already been paid for and covered with the blood of Jesus. Then turn from any sins that entangle you. Sometimes the devil tries to get us into the guilt and shame mode to make us think there is no point in striving to live our lives according to the Word of God. He doesn't have to do it blatantly either. He can just plant a seed, a little nagging thought, a memory of a former transgression. Don't let him in, keep reminding him, "not guilty." Jesus doesn't condemn you and neither can Satan.

Psalm 103:12

12He has removed our sins as far from us as the east is from the west.

Holy Father thank you that the moment we ask for your forgiveness you have removed every sin we have ever committed as far from us as the east is from the west. Help us each to continue in that freedom and endeavor to walk, live and conduct ourselves in a manner worthy of you, desiring to please you in all things and bearing fruit in every good work. Let your Word and your promises be manifested in our lives that we may not live condemned or with the burden of shame and regret.

Chapter 7
Depression

I am not an authority on the subject of depression, nor do I claim to have ever struggled with it. However, I do know what it means for your mind to go to dark places. I have experienced the overwhelming feeling of darkness, despair, and hopelessness many times in my life. It is not a comfortable experience to say the least. When I think back on particular times in my life, I sometimes wonder how I have any sanity at all. I also stand in wonder and awe at the amazing grace of the God I serve to allow me to be where I am today. I believe happiness is a choice. I believe the joy of the Lord is my strength, because He tells me it is. I believe depression can be overcome with praise, prayer and taking our thoughts captive to the obedience of God.

When I was walking through some of the darkest times of my life in a relationship that was toxic and tumultuous, I always clung to the promises of God whether or not I was living like a

Christian. I tolerated a way of life, being treated in a manner nobody who knows me would ever believe. I praise God for loving me enough not to leave me in the muck and the mire, and see me through that time. When I was facing that darkness, I felt as though all my prayers had been futile and wasn't sure God was ever going to fulfill any of His promises for me.

I am fortunate to have been blessed with a grandson during that dark time of my life who has brought more light, laughter, and joy to me than I could have ever imagined. I am certain God timed his birth just right for me and for my son, because He knows exactly what we need and when we need it. I would spend hours holding my grandson when he was an infant, simply soaking in every ounce of love. He's seven years old now, and he still loves coming to see Gammy. And my son, well, having his own son gave him a reason to live.

I have never been diagnosed with depression or clinical depression, but I know it is a very real thing. I also know God gives us the remedy in His Word. I'm not saying there aren't those who need medication, because I know there are. Chemical imbalance is a real thing. However, if you're struggling right now to "put on a happy face" or you're in a situation you feel is hopeless, I encourage you to take up the "Sword of the Spirit" which is the Word of God and wield it in defense.

2 Corinthians 10:3-5 (ESV)
³ For though we walk in the flesh, we are not waging war according to the flesh. ⁴ For the weapons of our warfare are not of the flesh but have divine power to destroy strongholds. ⁵ We destroy arguments and every lofty opinion raised against the knowledge of God, and take every thought captive to obey Christ

When we take up God's Word it helps us to destroy strongholds, arguments and every lofty opinion raised against the knowledge of God. It's easy to get lost in the muck and mire if we are not intentional about taking control of our thoughts, instead of letting our thoughts control us. When you find yourself in the heat of the battle with thoughts that are not conducive to your well-being put on some praise music and get your Bible out. That's the only way to do battle. I have often found listening to secular music takes me back to times and places emotionally and mentally that are not good for me and are rather dark. When I feel that danger, I make it a point to listen only to praise and worship music. It is the only music that does not remind me of things, times, places and even people of whom I do not want to be reminded. Please remember that Lucifer was the minister of music in heaven before the fall. Therefore, he will use music today to bombard our thoughts with evil, darkness, and sadness if we allow him to do so.

Isaiah 61:1-3 (KJV)
1 "The Spirit of the Lord God is upon Me, because the Lord hath anointed Me to preach good tidings unto the meek. He hath sent me to bind up the brokenhearted, to proclaim liberty to the captives, and the opening of the prison to them that are bound, 2 To proclaim the acceptable year of the Lord, and the day of vengeance of our God; to

comfort all that mourn,³ To appoint unto them that mourn in Zion, to give unto them beauty for ashes, the oil of joy for mourning, the garment of praise for the spirit of heaviness, that they might be called trees of righteousness, the planting of the Lord, that He might be glorified."

In Isaiah 61 we are reminded that Jesus will bind up the wounds of our broken hearts and set us free from our bondage. He will also give us beauty for ashes and a garment of praise that will lift the spirit of heaviness. This means, if we lift up His name in praise and worship, He will lift the spirit of heaviness or depression from us. The Bible also tells us we have the power of life and death in our tongue in *Proverbs 18:21*. Use your tongue for life, for praise, and to glorify the only wise God. Give Him the praise, honor, and glory due Him.

I believe when we purpose in our hearts to identify all the ways we are blessed, and all the things we have to be thankful for, the spirit of depression flees. I encourage you to find comfort, rest, peace and joy in the fullness of the presence of

God that is found when ushering in His spirit with praise.

Father forgive us when we lose sight of you and your goodness. When we feel the spirit of heaviness overcome us, please help us to be mindful to usher in your presence with praise and worship so that it must flee.

Chapter 8
Making Agreement with the Enemy

As believers in the Lord Jesus Christ we often cling to the promises in His word. One of the most used verses regarding prayer and agreement is Matthew 18:19. Sometimes we believe God will do exactly as we ask if we agree in prayer with someone. Other times we believe He can, but doubt that He will do it for us.

Matthew 18:19 (AMP)
19 Again I tell you, if two of you on earth agree (harmonize together, make a symphony together) about whatever [anything and everything] they may ask, it will come to pass and be done for them by My Father in heaven.

Proverbs 18:20-21 (NASB)
20 With the fruit of a man's mouth his stomach will be satisfied; He will be satisfied with the product of his lips. 21 Death and life are in the power of the

tongue,

And those who love it will eat its fruit.

What I want to share now is about making agreements. Because while agreeing together in prayer to see God move mightily is an awesome thing, I want you to know that there are other types of agreements as well.

If you have struggled in some area of your life with getting an answer from God or getting the answer that you know is His will according to what His Word promises, it may be that you've made an agreement with the enemy and his lies. Satan will always try to thwart the plans and purpose of God in your life and the lives of your family members.

When we make statements such as "This or that will never happen for me" for example, we are agreeing with the lies of the enemy. I have realized this predicament in my own life regarding things I have struggled with. When you find yourself asking God "Why is this happening?" or "Why isn't that happening?" I challenge you to take a look at your confessions and agreements. There is power in the words we speak. God created us in His image which means our words are powerful! He created the world and everything in it with the spoken word. In fact, as referenced earlier Proverbs 18:21 tells us we have the power of life and death in our tongue.

I have had to ask God to forgive me for agreeing with the enemy about situations in my life that never seemed to change and ask Him to break and sever every agreement I've made with the enemy. I can tell you from first-hand personal experience, I have seen His hand move mightily and rapidly by praying those words.

Again, if you have been praying about a particular issue for some time and it seems God is not listening, not hearing, or not answering please look at what you've been confessing. Many times, we do not realize we have made agreement with the enemy. Start confessing the promises of God and what He says about who you are and deny the enemy any entrance into or hold on your life. Ask Him to break those agreements you may have unwittingly made with the enemy and watch His hand move in your life. Start calling those things that are not as though they were. Start thinking on those things that are good, pure, noble, lovely, perfect, just and of good report.

Jesus said He came that we might have and enjoy abundant life and I believe he meant for that abundant life to be lived in the here and now. Yes, He also said we would have trials and tribulations, but exhorts us to "be of good cheer for He has already overcome the world," and He will help us to do the same.

Psalm 19:14 (NASB)
14 Let the words of my mouth and the meditation of my heart be acceptable in Your sight, O Lord, my rock and my Redeemer.

Philippians 4:8 (NIV)
8 Finally, brothers and sisters, whatever is true, whatever is noble, whatever is right, whatever is pure, whatever is lovely, whatever is admirable—if anything is excellent or praiseworthy—think about such things.

Romans 4:16-17 (AMP)

[16] Therefore, [inheriting] the promise is the outcome of faith and depends [entirely] on faith, in order that it might be given as an act of grace (unmerited favor), to make it stable and valid and guaranteed to all his descendants—not only to the devotees and adherents of the Law, but also to those who share the faith of Abraham, who is [thus] the father of us all. [17] As it is written, I have made you the father of many nations. [He was appointed our father] in the sight of God in Whom he believed, Who gives life to the dead and speaks of the nonexistent things that [He has foretold and promised] as if they [already] existed.

Father God let the words of our mouths and the meditation of our hearts be acceptable and pleasing in your sight. Fill us to overflowing with Your love and Your spirit and help us to think on those things that are good, pure, noble, lovely just, perfect and of good report. Help us to call those things that are not as though they were. Help us to be mindful of our thoughts and words so that we stay in agreement with Your Word. In the precious name of Jesus.

Chapter 9

Controlling Your Mind....

Instead of Allowing Your Mind to Control You

THE LIFE WE LEAD IS CREATED BY THE THOUGHTS WE THINK. IF WE WOULD LIKE TO IMPROVE OUR LIVES WE WILL HAVE TO IMPROVE OUR THOUGHTS.

The Bible has a lot to say about our thoughts, our mind, what we think about, and what we focus on. In **Proverbs 23:7** the Bible says, *"for as he thinks in his heart, so he is."* Eventually you will become what you think. You can't concentrate your focus and thoughts on one thing and become something else. If you allow yourself to think negative, worried, fearful thoughts then you will become a negative, worried, fearful person. You cannot expect victory if what you're dwelling on is defeat. You can't concentrate on the worst and expect the best.

You must be extremely careful and aware of what you allow your mind to think about. You must also be mindful of what you choose to dwell on.

Philippians 4:6-8 (NIV)
6 Do not be anxious about anything, but in every situation, by prayer and petition, with thanksgiving, present your requests to God. 7 And the peace of God, which transcends all understanding, will guard your hearts and your minds in Christ Jesus. 8 Finally, brothers and sisters, whatever is true, whatever is noble, whatever is right, whatever is pure, whatever is lovely, whatever is admirable—if anything is excellent or praiseworthy—think about such things.

Luke 21:13-15 (NIV)
13 And so you will bear testimony to me. 14 But make up your mind not to worry beforehand how you will defend yourselves. 15 For I will give you words and wisdom that none of your adversaries will be able to resist or contradict.

Fear is as strong as faith. If you give into fear and dwell on negative worst-case scenarios, you may start to act on it. Fear can actually bring things to pass just like faith can. Job said, *"the thing I greatly feared came upon me."* We have to make up our minds not to worry according to the Word of God. I know full well it is easier said than done, but when your fear is overcoming your faith get into the word of God. Read it out loud so your ears can hear. According to Romans 10:17 faith comes by hearing the Word of God.

The Bible clearly tells us what we should dwell on in Philippians 4:8; we are to think about those things that are true, noble, right, pure, lovely, admirable, excellent, and praiseworthy. Think about things that build you up, not tear you down. Think about all the great things God has done for you. In other words, you've got to dwell on the positive and not the negative. Stop thinking about what you don't have, and start thinking about what you do have. Stop thinking about what's wrong with you and start thinking about what's right with you. Stop thinking about how big your problem is and start dwelling on how big your God is.

If you're continually thinking about the goodness of God, you're not going to have any time to worry and complain and get down and discouraged. If you're always meditating on God's promises, then you're always going to be filled with a good report. The words that come out of your mouth are going to be faith-filled words, not fear filled words of worry, doubt and dread.

Psalm 139:1-3
1 You have searched me, LORD, and you know me. 2 You know when I sit and when I rise; you perceive my thoughts from afar. 3 You discern my going out and my lying down; you are familiar with all my ways.

God knows your thoughts and He's familiar with all your ways. So practice thinking on those things that are good, true, noble, lovely, just and of good report. I believe you will not regret it.

Chapter 10

Letting Go of the Past

Isaiah 42:8 (AMP)

"I am the LORD, that is My name; I will not give My glory to another, Nor My praise to graven images. 9) "Behold, the former things have come to pass, now I declare new things; before they spring forth I proclaim them to you."

Isaiah 43:18-19 (AMP)

18Do not [earnestly] remember the former things; neither consider the things of old. 19 Behold, I am doing a new thing! Now it springs forth; do you not perceive and know it and will you not give heed to it? I will even make a way in the wilderness and rivers in the desert.

There is a distinct theme in those scriptures. When God is preparing you for a new thing, He wants to do in your life He does not want you dwelling on the things of the past. You cannot start the next chapter of your life if you are always re-

reading the last one. How can you expect God to do something new for you if you are not actively looking forward?

Matthew 6:14
For if you forgive people their trespasses [their reckless and willful sins, leaving them, letting them go, and giving up resentment], your heavenly Father will also forgive you. [15]But if you do not forgive others their trespasses [their reckless and willful sins, leaving them, letting them go, and giving up resentment], neither will your Father forgive you your trespasses.

According to Matthew we must be willing to forgive others of their sins against us in order to be forgiven. We must be willing to let go and give up or release any resentment we have toward them. The following passage in Mark reiterates this further.

Mark 11:24-26

For this reason, I am telling you, whatever you ask for in prayer, believe (trust and be confident) that it is granted to you, and you will [get it]. 25And whenever you stand praying, if you have anything against anyone, forgive him and let it drop (leave it, let it go), in order that your Father Who is in heaven may also forgive you your [own] failings and shortcomings and let them drop. 26But if you do not forgive, neither will your Father in heaven forgive your failings and shortcomings.

Do you struggle with memories of the past? Do you have a hard time letting go of pain that was incurred weeks, months, even years ago? Do you have a hard time forgiving others and letting go of the wrongs done to you? I'm certain we all have those struggles at some point in our lives, but look what God does in Psalm 32:51.

Ps. 32:5I (AMP)

I acknowledged my sin to You, and my iniquity I did not hide. I said, I will confess my transgressions to the Lord [continually unfolding the past till all is told]--then You [instantly] forgave me the guilt and iniquity of my sin. Selah [pause, and calmly think of that]

When we acknowledge our sins, confess our transgressions and do not try to hide them, God forgives us instantly! Unfortunately, God did not give us the ability to forget the way He does whenever we ask forgiveness for our sins. Yet He has commanded us to forgive and let go of the wrongs done to us. I am a firm believer that He does not command us to do anything He does not also give us the ability to do.

If you're still struggling with unforgiveness and releasing the past it's time to start seeking first the Kingdom of God and His Righteousness and trusting in the Lord with all your heart, not leaning on your own understanding. There are some questions that will never be answered this side of eternity. It is not prudent to question God in His sovereignty as His ways are higher than ours, His thoughts are not our thoughts and His timing is not our timing. Our finite minds cannot begin to comprehend an infinite God. He does not require us to understand Him, but rather to trust Him. Put your faith, hope and trust in the only living God. He is your refuge and ever-present help in times of trouble. He can make a way when there seems to be no way. He works in ways we cannot see, and He will make a way if you will trust Him. He is able to do far over and exceedingly above anything that we ask, think or could ever possibly imagine. He has promised to perfect everything that concerns you and cause all things to work together for your good. Do you trust Him?

Sometimes we feel like hamsters running on the wheel of life. Running and running and running, but never really getting anywhere. We become frustrated and discontent because we can't find our way or discern which direction God wants us to go. There are some things however, we do not need to go to the "prayer closet" for to seek His guidance and direction. They are the things we already know are right to do; those things He already addresses in His Word, the things we sometimes overlook or choose not to address because it is not what we want to do. We predetermine in our own hearts and minds that our behavior is justified because we have been wronged. We decide that we have the right to hate this person or not forgive that person because of what they did to us. But that is not what God tells us to do. He tells us to forgive, that we might be forgiven. He tells us to love our enemies and bless them, bless and do not curse. He tells us not to return evil for evil, but to overcome evil with good. And what about when it's not someone you perceive as your enemy but in fact someone that you love or care about very much? Will you choose to let go of that unforgiveness, bitterness, anger, rage, malice, jealousy and whatever other negative thoughts or feelings you might have toward that person? Or will you hold on to those things and let them destroy your relationship? Don't misunderstand me here. There are times when circumstances are such that someone is in an abusive relationship from which they need to depart. God does not ask us to stay in those situations, but He does still want us to forgive. Forgiveness does not mean however, that you condone someone's actions, it simply means you will not let their actions negatively affect you and your future because you choose to let go. In cases where there is abuse, you usually also have to choose to let go of the person who is abusing unless they seek and find the help they need to stop being the abuser.

Holding on to unforgiveness, bitterness, resentment, anger, rage, or malice toward anyone only serves to do you harm. In all likelihood the person you harbor these feelings toward, doesn't even know you feel that way. Whatever they may have done to hurt you may likely have been forgotten by them and they have moved on with their lives. Unforgiveness and bitterness are the only poisons that eat their own container. Holding onto these emotions God has clearly told you to let go of, wastes so much time and energy it is absolutely exhausting, mentally, physically and spiritually. Won't you place it in his hands, nail it to the cross, and take up his yoke instead? His yoke is easy, and His burden is light. You will find peace that passes all-natural reasoning and understanding if you will but place it in the capable hands of the Father.

Chapter 11
Forgiveness

I realize I spoke a lot about forgiveness in the last chapter, but there is definitely more that can be said about it. I cannot stress enough the importance of being able to forgive others. I cannot express the importance of not only learning how to effectively forgive others yourself, but also teaching your little ones to forgive as well. I have three ex-husbands. I chose to divorce each of them for varying reasons. To this day I do not hold any hard feelings toward any of them. I wish them all the very best in their lives. I hope they come to know and enjoy a relationship with God like I do. I often pray for them because that is what God would have me do, and two of them are fathers to my children. One is a grandfather to my grandson. I can't say I have any "feelings" about them one way or the other. And while each has said many not nice and untrue things about me, I realize they will have to answer for that one day. It is not my problem, nor do I have to explain their viewpoints or defend mine.

I am very fortunate God has given me an uncanny ability to suppress things in my past that do not benefit me in my present. It doesn't do anyone any good to constantly dwell on the hurtful actions of another.

At the time I divorced my first husband who is the father of my twin sons, attending a parenting class for children of divorce was not required by the courts. Six years after our divorce we went back to court over child support issues and because we had never taken the class we were required to at that time. I remember thinking as I sat in class "I've been doing this for six years already, I could teach this class." It was very frustrating to have to take a class on something you were already doing. At the same time, if their father listened when he went to take the class, he may have learned something, I'm not sure. My children didn't always tell me the things their respective fathers would say to them about me, but sometimes they would. It must have been very confusing for them to have their fathers saying things they knew were not true, because they lived with me the majority of the time. While I knew that both my ex-husbands did this, I consistently refused to say derogatory things about them to my children. I knew one day they would see the truth without me ever saying a thing. My children are all grown-up now, and I can say without hesitation that I did exactly the right thing. I have no regrets about how I handled that issue, because they have reaped the fruit of the seeds they sowed and so have I. Today I enjoy rich, full relationships with all my children. The happiest times in my life over the last 7-10 years have been the times I get to hang out with them all together.

If you struggle with finding it in your heart to forgive someone in your life who has hurt you, please ask the Father to pierce and penetrate your heart, and create in you a heart that is soft, pliable, and moldable to His will. He will do it for you, and it is so freeing. You will not believe the weight you will feel lifted from you. I promise you will not regret it. God is faithful to forgive our sins when we find it in our hearts to forgive others. He is able to do so much more than we could ever ask, think or possibly imagine in and through us if we will let him.

Matthew 6:14-15 (NLT)
14 "If you forgive those who sin against you, your heavenly Father will forgive you. 15 But if you refuse to forgive others, your Father will not forgive your sins.

Ephesian 3:20 (AMP)
20 Now to Him who is able to [carry out His purpose and] do superabundantly more than all that we dare ask or think [infinitely beyond our greatest prayers, hopes, or dreams], according to His power that is at work within us, 21 to Him be the glory in the church and in Christ Jesus throughout all generations forever and ever. Amen.

Ezekiel 36:26 (AMP)
26 Moreover, I will give you a new heart and put a new spirit within you, and I will remove the heart

of stone from your flesh and give you a heart of flesh.

Mark 9:24 (NLT)
[24] The father instantly cried out, "I do believe, but help me overcome my unbelief!"

Father I ask right now that anyone reading this who has been holding unforgiveness in their hearts would seek You for the faith to release it to You. Touch their hearts right now and pierce and penetrate, giving them soft, pliable and moldable hearts of flesh that are agreeable to your will. Help their unbelief Lord and draw them to you like a moth to the flame.

Frequently I find some people don't realize the help they have available to them through the power of prayer and asking God to help their unbelief. I am hopeful the previous verses touch hearts and minds and help them see and understand all God is willing and in fact desires to do for us His children.

Chapter 12
Mind Your Own Business

Psalm 37:1-5 (NLT)
¹ Don't worry about the wicked or envy those who
do wrong. ² For like grass, they soon fade away.
Like spring flowers, they soon wither. ³ Trust in the
Lord and do good. Then you will live safely in the
land and prosper. ⁴ Take delight in the Lord,
and he will give you your heart's desires. ⁵ Commit
everything you do to the Lord.
Trust him, and he will help you.

Have you ever wondered why some people seem to have all the luck? Why they seem to live a life of ease and prosperity and have everything they want, even if they are not servants of the Lord? I think it is human nature to think that way sometimes. We will always have questions like that while we are here on this earth because for whatever reason we seem to have some idea that life should be fair. The reality is life is not fair. Another reality is we should be minding our own business according to the Word of God. The Bible clearly tells us not to worry about the wicked or their prosperity. We are to put our faith and trust in God and trust Him to provide everything we need spiritually, mentally, physically, financially and emotionally. We can place our faith, hope, and trust in the only living God who has promised to take care of our needs.

James 4:1-3 (CEB)
¹What is the source of conflict among you? What is the source of your disputes? Don't they come from your cravings that are at war in your own lives? ² You long for something you don't have, so you commit murder. You are jealous for something you can't get, so you struggle and fight. You don't have because you don't ask. ³ You ask and don't have because you ask with evil intentions, to waste it on your own cravings.

According to this passage we don't have because we don't ask. Or, we ask and do not have because we ask with wrong motives. How often have you asked God for something or to do something with a wrong motive in your heart? Was the request to benefit the lust of your flesh, or to benefit someone else? Was it to help you be a more faithful servant of God? Sometimes we don't get what we think we want simply because God knows better than us and is protecting us from a bad decision. Sometimes we don't get what we think we want because we want it more than we want God. God is a jealous God and He will have no other gods before him. So, if you placed more importance on something or someone in your life don't expect to keep it or them. God will not allow us to have idols placed before Him in our lives.

I know it is tempting to also compare ourselves to others and wonder why they seem to have everything they want in life when we may feel like we are struggling to make it through each day. First of all, things are not always what they seem. Sometimes those that you are feeling so envious or jealous of are having struggles of their own that you know nothing about. People often put on a front to hide what their life is really like. What you see on Facebook, Instagram and Twitter are only glimpses of people's lives. They don't tell the true story of any person's life. So, stop comparing yourself and stop asking God "Why them and not me?"

Romans 9:14-16, 18, 20 (CEB)
14 So what are we going to say? Isn't this unfair on God's part? Absolutely not! 15 He says to Moses, I'll have mercy on whomever I choose to have mercy, and I'll show compassion to whomever I choose to show compassion. 16 So then, it doesn't depend on a person's desire or effort. It depends entirely on God, who shows mercy.
18 So then, God has mercy on whomever he wants to, but he makes resistant whomever he wants to. 20 You are only a human being. Who do you think you are to talk back to God? Does the clay say to the potter, "Why did you make me like this?"

The title of this chapter is "Mind Your Own Business" and I personally have an aversion to people who don't do just that. Apparently, God has the same aversion according to the message in the passage above. It is not our place to question God or His sovereignty. As we look to Jesus and keep our eyes fixed and focused on Him, delighting ourselves in Him, He will give us the desires of our hearts. If you are wondering why your life is not as easy or as good or as blessed as someone else's you need to adjust your sight and fix your gaze on the Giver instead of the gifts someone else has. It's sort of akin to when your children (if you have children) think you're supposed to do every single thing for them equally when they have varying needs at varying times in their lives. They do not always need the same thing at the same time and neither do we.

If we are about the business of loving as we have been commanded to love, we won't have time to be worried about what somebody else has that we don't. Get busy loving people and loving God. Get your eyes fixed and focused on Him. Make sure that you want a relationship with the Creator more than you want any other thing in your life. Then you won't have time to be worried about what somebody else has that you don't. After all love does not envy.

Father fill us to overflowing with your light and your love. Let us be conduits through which they flow to others. Help us to keep our eyes fixed and focused on you so that we might love others as you have loved us rather than envying them. Help us to understand that you give us each exactly what we need when we need it.

Chapter 13

Give Thanks with a Grateful Heart

I am not sure know about you, but when I think of all the things God has done for me, I can't help but give humble thanks to Him. We have so much to be grateful for each and every day. The very air that we breathe is a reason to give Him thanks. Without God we are nothing, we can do nothing we can be nothing. In Him we live and move and have our being.

Do you wake up each morning and find something to give God thanks for? He's a good, good Father and lavishes blessings on us all the time. Often, we do not recognize them if we are not paying attention. I find it extremely bothersome to be around people who only see the bad things in life. They seem to never take the time to acknowledge all the wonderful things they have experienced. If one is constantly focused on negative things, they can expect to have a negative life, as continuous negative thoughts will never produce a positive life.

Jesus Christ died on a cross to save us from our sins and reconcile us to the Father. If they (Father, Son, and Holy Spirit) never did another thing for you or me, that sacrifice alone would be more than enough. God wants us to come to a point in our walk with Him of recognizing, He is more than enough to meet every single need that we have. He is our Provider, Healer, Savior, Redeemer, and Friend who sticks closer than a brother. He is always with us. King of kings, Lord of lords, Prince of Peace, that's our God and there is nothing He cannot do in, to, and through each of us.

If you want more of God in your life start lifting your voice in praise and worship thanking Him for his goodness, mercies, and grace He so lavishly showers on each of us. Praise and worship usher in the presence of the Holy Spirit. We are instructed repeatedly in the scriptures to give thanks. I encourage you to start every day with a list of the things you are grateful for, reminding yourself of all God has done for you.

Let the following scriptures be a guide for you to use.

1 Thessalonians 5:18 (NIV)
give thanks in all circumstances; for this is God's
will for you in Christ Jesus.

Psalm 107:1 & 8 (NIV)
¹Give thanks to the Lord, for he is good; his love
endures forever.
⁸Let them give thanks to the Lord for his unfailing
love and his wonderful deeds for mankind

According to the Bible, God's love never fails;
it endures forever. Jesus Christ is the same
yesterday, today, and forever according to Hebrews
13:8. Therefore, every single day and in every
circumstance, we are to give thanks to God for He
is good, His love never ends or fails. Thank Him for
all His wonderful deeds. The Bible says in Romans
8:28 that "He is working everything together for
good for those who love Him and are called
according to His purpose." That means even when
you can't see it or feel it God is working on your

behalf to perfect every single thing that concerns you.

The more you find to give thanks for, the more reason you will have to be thankful. Recognizing your blessings is the first step to having and maintaining a grateful heart. God wants to bless us and give us abundant lives. However, we must come to a point of desiring the Giver more than we desire the gifts. Nothing else really matters if we don't have Him. When your heart's desire becomes to be caught up in His presence, you will not long for anything or anyone else. God wants us to crave relationship with Him above everything else in our lives. He will have no other gods before Him.

Father, forgive us when we place anything or anyone else before You in our lives. Please give us a hunger and thirst to know You more. Search our hearts and see if there is any wicked way in us and lead us in your way everlasting. Create in us a clean heart and renew a steadfast and loyal spirit within us that seeks to chase hard after You, giving thanks for all You have done and continue to do.

Chapter 14

God is in the Little Things

1 Peter 5:6-8 (NIV)

[6] Humble yourselves, therefore, under God's mighty hand, that he may lift you up in due time. [7] Cast all your anxiety on him because he cares for you. [8] Be alert and of sober mind. Your enemy the devil prowls around like a roaring lion looking for someone to devour.

Do you ever wonder if your prayers are being heard? Of course we all do at times. Do you ever ask the Lord just to show you a glimpse of His hand, just so you know He's still there, still listening?

During a certain period of my life, the Lord told me repeatedly to be still and know that He is still God, still on the throne. He told me to trust Him because He holds my future in His perfectly capable hands. Over and over again I cast all my cares at His feet, only to pick them back up. His Word promises that He will perfect everything that concerns me; therefore, I can relax and let Him handle everything, because after all He is in control anyway, not me.

One morning as I read the Word and conveyed my prayers in my prayer journal, I asked Him once again to show me His hand, to let me see He's listening and I was being heard. I don't know about the rest of you, but it's HARD for me to be still and trust He's working on my behalf to perfect everything that concerns me. It's hard to put faith into practice, but alas, faith without works is dead right?

James 2:17-19 NIV 17 In the same way, faith by itself, if it is not accompanied by action, is dead. 18 But someone will say, "You have faith; I have deeds." Show me your faith without deeds, and I will show you my faith by my deeds.

We can have head knowledge about Who God is and what He is capable of, yet still not believe He will do what He says. When we do this we're virtually tying His hands.

Back to my morning... After dropping my daughter off at school that morning and leaving the high school parking lot, my accelerator reach 35 mph in the 20 mph school zone. I was pulled over by a police officer. As I was in the process of pulling into the Kroger parking lot, I told God I needed His favor in the situation. I proceeded to roll my window down and hand the officer my documents. As I was fumbling to find my most recent insurance card, I realized it must still be on my dresser at home as the one in my car had expired. He asked if my insurance was current, and I told him it was and he then asked when I had gotten a ticket last. I told him I thought it had been a year and a half or two years. Officer McCoy then went back to his car. When he came back to my window these were his words, "I don't know what's gotten into me this morning because I don't usually just give warnings for 15 over in a school zone; however, I'm just going to give you a warning today and ask you to slow down. It won't cost you anything and you won't have to go to court, but I do need you to slow down." I said, "I can tell you what got into you Officer McCoy, I prayed for favor." He responded with a smile, "Maybe it was divine intervention." And indeed it was God's favor and divine intervention that kept me from getting an official ticket that morning.

Did I mention it was very foggy that morning, resulting in heavier than usual traffic? And, as I drove out of the Kroger parking lot, I realized I would have to stop to get gas before heading for the interstate and the rest of my commute to work. As I pulled the nozzle on the gas pump to my car I once again sought the Lord, *"God, I need you to go before me and clear out the traffic this morning so I can still get to work on time."* My usual arrival time was 8:30...I walked into my office at 8:35 that morning. God is good, all the time, and He is concerned about every little detail of your life, no matter how insignificant you may think it is. And if He's that concerned about the little things, the big things you've been praying about for years surely have answers on the way! He is able to do far over and exceedingly above anything we can ask, think or could even possibly

imagine! However, His ways are not our ways, and
His thoughts are not our thoughts, and His timing
is most assuredly not our timing. But nothing is
too difficult for the God of this universe who knew
me before He knit me in my mother's womb.

Chapter 15
Fear/Worry/Dread

2 Timothy 1:7 (AMP)
For God did not give us a spirit of timidity (of cowardice, of craven and cringing and fawning fear), but [He has given us a spirit] of power and of love and of calm and well-balanced mind and discipline and self-control.

Like everyone, I have had plenty of opportunity to live in fear and worry throughout my lifetime. However, it is not God's will for us to do so. How do you handle fear when it comes knocking on your door? I am very fortunate that I grew up with a mother who drilled into my head and my heart, 2 Timothy 1:7. Because of the drilling there have not been too many times that I have been afraid of anything. That being the case I find it a little difficult to identify with those who walk and live in fear, worry, and dread on a routine basis. I love to reassure them that God has got their back. My favorite question to ask someone who is afraid is, "What's the worst thing that could happen?" "Will you die?" If the answer is no, then what are you really afraid of?

I have three children and a grandson which in itself is enough to cause me all kinds of worry and fear if I chose to walk in it. I choose instead to stand on the Word of God that reassures me God is not the one giving me a spirit of fear. Instead He gives me a spirit of love and a sound, well-balanced mind.

I have worked with the same organization for 31 years now. Through the years, every single year until 2019 we have had to fight for the money to exist. The company I work for is a city government-owned organization and therefore subject to budgeting constraints. I have watched people come and go over the years and yes some of them left out of fear of the unknown when budget time rolled around. For those who have worked the closest to me, I have always assured them that God is my provider and theirs too. As long as He chooses to use our organization to meet our needs as well as the needs of the uninsured/underinsured sick population of our community, we will receive the funding needed and our doors will remain open. I have never been afraid in those instances even though I had no idea where I might seek employment if the doors were to close. It has been all I have known my entire adult life.

Luke 12:32
Do not be seized with alarm and struck with fear, little flock, for it is your Father's good pleasure to give you the kingdom!

Wow! Did you read that? God delights in providing for us. He owns everything and it is his "good pleasure to give you the kingdom!" So why would I worry or live in fear when I know He is watching over me and knows my needs before I even ask.

What fears do you hold in your heart today? Do you know how to ease them and live in peace? I would encourage you to meditate on the Word of God and what He has to say about fear.

John 14:27 (AMP)

Peace I leave with you; My [own] peace I now give
and bequeath to you. Not as the world gives do I
give to you. Do not let your hearts be troubled,
neither let them be afraid. [Stop allowing
yourselves to be agitated and disturbed; and do not
permit yourselves to be fearful and intimidated and
cowardly and unsettled.]

Rest in the assurance of a loving God and do
not be fearful or intimidated. Satan would love for
you to be bound up in fear. That's how he gains
control. People have a tendency to do some pretty
crazy things out of fear. They may lie, push others
away, run, hide, behave poorly and lash out at
others because of fear. Usually the first question I
ask myself when someone is acting out of the norm
and exhibiting bad behavior is, "what are they
afraid of?"

Is there anything in your life that has you
afraid? Whether it is fear of showing your true
feelings for someone or taking some other type of
risk you can seek your Heavenly Father for peace

and let not your heart be troubled. He is faithful to provide the calm of a sound, well-balanced mind in the midst of your fears.

Nobody can control what others do or omit doing. Worry and fear will not change that fact. Trust in the Lord. Don't count on your own understanding. When something doesn't seem right to me and I can't seem to grasp a clear understanding of the situation, I have learned to say, "I trust you God, I know your timing is perfect." God tells us His ways are not our ways and His thoughts are not our thoughts. However, when we learn to place our faith and trust in Him, we begin to rest in His promises because we learn that He is faithful to fulfill them.

Chapter 16
Peace in Trusting

When Jesus departed the earth to ascend into heaven to sit at the right hand of the Father, He promised to leave the disciples with His peace. He noted it was not the same peace the world gives. He left them with peace that would help them not to worry or be afraid. As believers in and followers of the Lord Jesus Christ we have the same peace available to us.

John 14:26-28 (NIV)
26 But the Advocate, the Holy Spirit, whom the Father will send in my name, will teach you all things and will remind you of everything I have said to you. 27 Peace I leave with you; my peace I give you. I do not give to you as the world gives. Do not let your hearts be troubled and do not be afraid.

The peace God offers requires faith and trust in Him. We must train our minds to be unwavering and actively trust. When we try to understand some things ourselves that are not meant for our understanding we can get caught in a trap, and as a result not, live in the peace He offers. God requires whole-hearted trust and faith in Him and His promises.

Isaiah 26:3-4 (NIV)
3 You will keep in perfect peace those whose minds are steadfast, because they trust in you. 4 Trust in the LORD forever, for the LORD, the LORD himself, is the Rock eternal.

Proverbs 3:5-6 (NIV)
5 Trust in the LORD with all your heart and lean not on your own understanding;
6 in all your ways submit to him, and he will make your paths straight.

Often, we do not live in peace because we are living in fear. If we are allowing God's perfect love to manifest in our lives there should be no fear, because His perfect love drives out fear. God gives us a spirit of power, love and a sound, well-balanced mind.

1 John 4:18 (NIV)
18 There is no fear in love. But perfect love drives out fear, because fear has to do with punishment. The one who fears is not made perfect in love.

2 Timothy 1:7 (NKJV)
7 For God has not given us a spirit of fear, but of power and of love and of a sound mind.

For many years Satan tried to bind me up with fear and anxiety. As I mentioned in the previous chapter my mother often quoted 2 Timothy 1:7 to me. This verse has stuck with me over the years in every fearful situation. It is not God's will for us to live in fear and anxiety, or to worry all the time. He came that we might have and enjoy an abundant life. Granted, a life of abundance comes in varying fashions as God blesses us in many ways.

I clung to the word of God for over 2.5 years praying for and seeking His guidance, wisdom, and direction in my life. I often wondered whether He was listening. I often wondered what exactly His plan for my life is and what purpose He would accomplish through me. I also choose to speak daily "I trust You God, to perfect everything that concerns me and my children." I believe there is tremendous power in our words. He tells us we have the power of life and death in our tongues. I believe when we speak the Word of God over our lives we are speaking life to ourselves and those we love.

So many times, God has spoken to my spirit and told me to be still and know He is God. Often, I have laid my problems and worries at the foot of the cross only to take them back up again. So I have to speak again, "I trust You Lord with all my heart and I will not lean on my own finite understanding of an amazingly infinite God. I know Your ways are higher than mine and Your thoughts are not my thoughts. Thank You that Your plan is to do me good and not harm, to give me hope and a future. Thank You that surely there is a future and my hope will not be cut off. Thank You that You will give me the desires of my heart; make Your desires my desires Lord. Let Your will and Your way be done in my life today and every day."

I'm not sure why God has placed it on my heart to share these particular things with you except perhaps to encourage someone else who might struggle with trusting God.

I believe God is faithful to perform His word, but I also believe we have to get out of the way sometimes in order for Him to do so. And sometimes we think we have a situation handled when we really don't. Sometimes we waste so much time and energy trying to fix a situation that is not in our power or authority to fix. It must be placed in God's hands and left there in order for Him to accomplish what He wants to accomplish, and not what we want to see accomplished. His ways are not our ways. His thoughts are not our thoughts. And His timing is most assuredly not our timing. We live in such a microwave, instant gratification society these days we often want God to "hurry up and do something" when all along He's waiting patiently for us to get out of the way so He can. He will keep in perfect peace those whose minds are steadfast because they trust in Him. We can trust Him because the one who has promised is faithful.

I encourage you today to lay whatever worries, troubles, or fears you may have at the foot of the Cross and leave them there. Do not pick them up again and take them upon yourself. God is able to do far over and exceedingly above anything you can ask, think, or even possibly imagine. Let Him work in your life, He's waiting for you to let go of the reins so He can steer for a while.

Chapter 17
Hope

There are, a myriad of scriptural references related to hope. Resoundingly the message is to put our hope, faith, and trust in God. However, how often do we put our hope, faith, and trust in man and what he can do, knowing all along man can do nothing without the very breath of God in him. Why do we look to others to fulfill our dreams, hopes, and expectations? God is the only One who will never leave us or forsake us. He is the only One who will never fail us. We should place our faith, hope, confidence, and trust in the hands of the only wise God who is able to do far over and exceedingly above all we dare ask, think or even possibly imagine.

On a personal level I can tell you I have experienced a lot of disappointment throughout different periods of my life from various people for various reasons. What is the most predominant reason? Placing my hope and trust in man who is always subject to fail me or let me down because after all they are only human just like I am. When I have reached a point of feeling as though I have no hope for any given situation, I realize I have placed my hope in man, rather than in God. One is always subject to the pain of disappointment or rejection when they place their hopes and dreams in the hands of another human being.

God alone knows the plans He has for you, and they are to do you good and not harm, to give you hope and a future. His will is for you to have and enjoy an abundant life. The "thief" however, is still out there to lie, steal, kill, and destroy, going around like a roaring lion seeking whom he may devour. "May" in that verse indicates we have to give him permission to do so. Will you let him devour you? You have God given authority over him for your protection and the protection of your family, all you have to do is claim it through the blood of Jesus Christ.

I encourage you today to place your hope in the living God whose power no foe can withstand. After all if God is for us, who or what in the world can stand against us? Plead the blood of Jesus over yourself and every member of your family asking God to cause His supernatural favor to go before each of you in His sight and in the sight of man. Nothing is impossible with God and nothing is too difficult for Him. Sometimes however, we need to let go, and let God which is a very difficult thing to do. Control is an illusion and the only person we have control of is ourselves. God is in control...and we are either subject to Him or subject to the enemy. The only thing you have control over is your choices. Who are you going to allow to control your life?

Thank You Father God for the hope I have found in You, the Author and Perfecter of my faith. Thank you that I can put my faith, hope, and trust in the only living God. Thank You that You are able to do far over and exceedingly above anything I ask, think or could ever possibly imagine in, to, and through me. Make my life a living sacrifice, holy and acceptable to You Lord. Use me as You will and let me always keep my eyes on You and my faith, hope, and trust in You Lord, for You alone are worthy. In Jesus' precious name, Amen and so be it.

Chapter 18

Choose Life

I realize with a title like "Choose Life" you may automatically assume this is going to be a chapter about abortion...however, that is not so. I want to talk about choices. We all have them to make and make them every day. So often, people think they can keep doing the same thing over and over and expect they are going to see a different result. From what I've heard that behavior is the definition of insanity! If you want a better life you have to start making better choices. There is no way around that fact. Your life is a culmination of the choices you have made whether good, bad, or indifferent. This is what the Word of God tells us about our choices:

Deuteronomy 30:19
¹⁹I call heaven and earth to witness this day against you that I have set before you life and

death, the blessings and the curses; therefore
choose life, that you and your descendants may live

God gives us the choice between life and
death, blessings and curses, then He tells us to
CHOOSE LIFE! How does that work? Well, you
start by making choices related to your health and
sanity that bring life and health to you mentally,
physically, spiritually, and emotionally.

He also wants us to choose who we will
serve. One either makes the choice to serve God or
to serve Satan. There is no in between, for if you
choose not to serve God you are serving Satan by
default whether you think you are or not.

Joshua 24:15
15And if it seems evil to you to serve the Lord,
choose for yourselves this day whom you will serve,
whether the gods which your fathers served on the
other side of the River, or the gods of the Amorites,
in whose land you dwell; but as for me and my
house, we will serve the Lord.

Job 34:4

⁴Let us choose for ourselves that which is right; let us know among ourselves what is good.

Revelation 3:16

¹⁶So, because you are lukewarm and neither cold nor hot, I will spew you out of My mouth!

The Bible makes it clear if you are not choosing life and service to God you are indeed by default choosing death and a life of destruction. My challenge to you is this, if your life is not what or where you would like it to be, start making different and better choices. Choose life, choose service to God. Choose to surrender control of your life to Him for He who has promised is faithful to fulfill His promises.

James 1:12 (AMP)

¹²Blessed (happy, to be envied) is the man who is patient under trial and stands up under temptation, for when he has stood the test and

been approved, he will receive [the victor's] crown of life which God has promised to those who love Him.

1 John 2:25 (AMP)
[25]And this is what He Himself has promised us—the life, the eternal [life].

Chapter 19
NEVER ALONE

NEVER = not ever; at no time; not at all; absolutely not; to no extent or degree

God sent His Son Jesus to be with us. When Jesus ascended to heaven to be with the Father, the Holy Spirit was sent to live in us so we might never be alone. There is nowhere we can run or hide that He is not there in our midst. Though often we may try to hide the same way Adam and Eve did in the garden.

Psalm 139:7-12 (NIV)
7 Where can I go from your Spirit? Where can I flee from your presence? 8 If I go up to the heavens, you are there; if I make my bed in the depths, you are there. 9 If I rise on the wings of the dawn, if I settle on the far side of the sea, 10 even there your hand will guide me, your right hand will hold me fast. 11 If I say, "Surely the darkness will hide me and the light become night around me," 12 even the

darkness will not be dark to you; the night will shine like the day, for darkness is as light to you.

We do not have to be afraid or get discouraged because God has promised that we will never be alone. He will always be there to guide us.

Deuteronomy 31:8 (NIV)
8 The Lord himself goes before you and will be with you; he will never leave you nor forsake you. Do not be afraid; do not be discouraged."

God wants us to be content with what we have and not fall into the trap of chasing after money. He is our Provider and He will take care of us and never forsake us.

Hebrews 13:5 (NIV)
5 Keep your lives free from the love of money and be content with what you have, because God has said, "Never will I leave you; never will I forsake you."

Psalm 46:10 (AMP)

¹⁰ Let be and be still, and know (recognize and understand) that I am God. I will be exalted among the nations! I will be exalted in the earth!

Have you ever experienced a time of loneliness in your life? I think we all have at some time or another. It is during those deepest times of loneliness we sometimes reach a dark place within ourselves. Sometimes we look to fill that void with people or things that are not always best for us. For some it is a relationship with someone who is not healthy. For others they may try to fill the void with food or alcohol, or some other addictive substance. There are many ways we try to fill the void only God can fill. He promises to NEVER leave us or forsake us. So even when we are at the deepest, darkest, loneliest pit in our lives, He is there! His Word says so and I believe it. His Word says there is nowhere we can go to flee from His presence! That is an awesome thought to me, almost too great for my finite mind to grasp. Our God never leaves us! And what's the definition of never? Never = not ever; at no time; not at all; absolutely not; to no extent or degree!

Often when we are in the middle of a tumultuous relationship in which we are clearly "unequally yoked" (2 Corinthians 6:14) we wrestle with God about what to do and we may feel lost, chaotic, and confused. When all the while He's whispering to us "let be and be still and know that I am God" (Psalm 46:10). We wrestle with our thoughts, emotions, feelings and feel lonely, alone and distraught. And still He's whispering, "Let be, and be still." "I am with you always and I will never leave you or forsake you." Learning to "be still" takes time and patience with God and with yourself, but it is one of the most rewarding and freeing experiences you can have. If you will be consistent and persevere in your faith in what God is doing in you and in your circumstances. Pursue God and everything else will fall into place. He is your Provider and He will provide every single thing you need spiritually, mentally, physically, emotionally, and financially. He's your Healer and He will bind up the wounds of your broken heart if

you will let him. So be still and know…He is God!
He loves you with an everlasting love! He is able to
do far over and exceedingly above all that you ask,
think or even dare to imagine in, to and through
you. Will you let him?

  You can do all things through Christ who
gives you strength, because His Word says you can
and His word is absolute truth.

Isaiah 26:3 (AMP)
3 You will guard him and keep him in perfect and
constant peace whose mind [both its inclination
and its character] is stayed on You, because he
commits himself to You, leans on You, and hopes
confidently in You.

  Where is your mind? Where are your
thoughts? Are you focused on God? Are you
committed to Him? Are you confident in Him,
trusting that His word is truth? He wants to give
you perfect peace. Will you let him?

John 16:33 (AMP)

33 I have told you these things, so that in Me you may have [perfect] peace and confidence. In the world you have tribulation and trials and distress and frustration; but be of good cheer [take courage; be confident, certain, undaunted]! For I have overcome the world. [I have deprived it of power to harm you and have conquered it for you.]

1 John 4:18 (NIV)
18 There is no fear in love. But perfect love drives out fear, because fear has to do with punishment. The one who fears is not made perfect in love.

If you are afraid to let God be in control, then choose to let His perfect love wash over you that it might drive out the fear inside. The fear of being alone may drive the chaos and confusion in your thoughts and emotions and cause you to cling tightly to what is not healthy for you spiritually, mentally or emotionally. It's God's will for you to prosper and be in good health, even as your soul prospers.

3 John 1:2 (NASB)

2 Beloved, I pray that in all respects you may prosper and be in good health, just as your soul prospers.

Believe me, I have on more than one occasion felt lost and confused as though I was living in chaos, because I couldn't figure out what was happening at the end of a relationship. It has been in those times I lost sight of the promise of Emanuel, God with us. It has been during those times I haven't completely fixed my hope on God and the things above. It has been during those times I was not delighting myself in the Lord, because I was fulfilling the lust of the flesh instead.

When one of the relationships I was in for 13-14 months, ended, I felt lost, and alone. I thought the guy I was dating was a "good guy" who would eventually "fall in love with me." Boy was I wrong. Not that he wasn't a good guy. He treated me well and I thought he loved me, but in the end he informed me he did not love me, and I was not what he wanted. It was a bit of a sucker punch to the gut, because what in the world are you doing dating someone for 13-14 months if you don't love them? Talk about feeling alone, unwanted, and unloved. I poured a lot of myself into that relationship and lost a lot of myself along the way. After it was over, I realized how much of myself I had given up to be with him.

I came to realize my life was much more peaceful without this man in it. I also realized I wanted to live in peace. I was going to be involved with someone, they would have to enhance that peace, or our relationship would not work. However, I was still doing things my way and ended up involved in another 13-month dead-end relationship. I did not wait for my heavenly Father to bring me the man he had for me. Since I didn't wait, and I believe I had a "broken picker," I ended up with someone with whom I was totally incompatible.

Unfortunately, coming out of that relationship, I still wasn't ready to surrender my hopes and dreams to the Father. I ended up dating a couple of different men that didn't work out. The reality is, through it all, I have never been alone. Jesus is a friend who sticks closer than a brother. When you don't feel Him near, it's not because he's gone anywhere, it's because you have moved out of His presence. The challenge is to keep your heart and mind fixed and focused on God.

Heavenly Father, I pray for those reading this chapter right now, who feel like they are alone in this life or alone in their struggles. I ask that You reach down and fill the void that only You can fill. Let them feel your presence so that they know unequivocally that they are never alone because You are always with them. Holy Spirit comfort them as only You can, and Jesus please bind up the wounds of their broken hearts as You promise to do. Help them to be still and know that you are God. Thank You Father for complete healing and restoration being manifested in them right now by the power of the blood and stripes of Jesus.

Chapter 20
Human Doings vs. Human Beings

I wonder how many of us get caught up in being "human doings" rather than human beings. Allow me to explain what I mean. I fear that too often believers get caught up in "service to the Lord" that He never called them to. Then they get worn out and burned out because they are "doing" what they think is expected of them. I think perhaps some believe that serving in every capacity they can, and being at church every time the doors open will help them be closer to God. The reality is nothing you do will get you closer to God than spending time with Him; praying and studying His word.

I spent a lot of years being a human doing. That's not to say those who serve in the various ministries of the church shouldn't serve. I'm not saying that at all. If you believe God has truly called you to serve in whatever capacity you may be serving at your home church you should absolutely continue with that service.

Often when we haven't performed perfectly in our lives and we've gotten off course with our faith it's easy to become a human doing. However, we cannot get back on track in our own power. We cannot make up for our mistake by trying to perform perfectly. Because the reality is that no matter how well we perform as human doings, we cannot ever out-perform the blood of Jesus on the Cross. The good news is, we don't have to because He already did it for us.

I can't help but believe that many become human doings out of fear. Fear that they are not good enough to receive the grace and mercy of our Father in Heaven. Therefore, they must work, and work, and work trying to perform perfectly so God will forgive them and love them.

Luke 10:38-40 (NIV)

38 As Jesus and his disciples were on their way, he came to a village where a woman named Martha opened her home to him. 39 She had a sister called Mary, who sat at the Lord's feet listening to what he said. 40 But Martha was distracted by all the preparations that had to be made. She came to him and asked, "Lord, don't you care that my sister has left me to do the work by myself? Tell her to help me!"

41 "Martha, Martha," the Lord answered, "you are worried and upset about many things, 42 but few things are needed—or indeed only one. Mary has chosen what is better, and it will not be taken away from her."

Martha was a human doing in this passage. She didn't even realize that all her busyness was so unnecessary.

Psalm 46:10 (NIV)
He says, "Be still, and know that I am God; I will be exalted among the nations, I will be exalted in the earth."

How can we be still if we are constantly in a state of motion? How can you ever hear God's still, small voice if you're never still long enough to listen?

I spent a lot of years serving in the local church. I'm not saying if you have gifts, talents, and abilities conducive to working in the local church that you shouldn't serve. What I am saying is that Believers... ALL Believers in Christ make up The Church. So wherever you are and whatever you're doing you should be representing Christ and sharing your faith in God. If you're a great singer, then help lead worship. If you're a fantastic teacher, please, go teach Sunday School or help in the Children's ministry. Whatever gift or talent God has blessed you with, use it for His glory in whatever way He leads you to do so. Don't wear yourself out or burn yourself out being a "Martha." Be a "Mary" instead, choosing the better thing, spending time in the Word of God and praying. Seeking His face rather than His hand.

During all the time I spent serving in various ministries of the church, I spent countless hours on the road getting there for all those events. I believe it might have been more useful to spend that time in my prayer closet, or reading and studying the Word with my family at home. I did what I felt was right at the time, but I have since learned, it is about relationship with the Father/Son/Holy Spirit, not about religion, rituals or unrealistic expectations. I'd rather be a human being, being still and knowing that He is God, than a human doing and not choosing that which is the better thing.

Chapter 21
The Do's and Don'ts

Exodus 20:2-17 sets forth the Old Testament Laws. What is the relevance of those words to our lives today? I mean does God really still expect us to live our lives this way? Some would ask, if it is even possible to live your life this way? Many offer that these words come from a different time and place than where we are today, and therefore not relevant to our lives. I would argue that these words are very relevant to our lives today. God's Word says in *Hebrews 13:8* that *"Jesus Christ is the same yesterday, today, and forever."* For me that means His Word is relevant to my life today, and every day in its entirety.

Here is the misnomer for most... People have a tendency to believe the Ten Commandments are somehow for God's benefit. Much like a teenager who thinks their parents rules are for their own benefit, rather than for their protection. That's the key.... learning and understanding God does not give us the "do's and don'ts" for His benefit. Think about it, what benefit would that be to Him? Just like when you tell your little one not to touch the hot surface of the stove. It's not because that would be of benefit to you, it's for their protection, to keep them from getting hurt.

Reflect on the do's and don'ts in your life. How many times have you ignored them? I know I have chosen to ignore them too many times to count in my own life. I also know that every single time I've ignored them, I've been hurt. God hates to see our pain, but sometimes it takes our pain and brokenness to bring us back to Him for our healing and restoration. He is a God of healing, restoration, and reconciliation. There is nowhere we can run that is too far from Him.

For several years after my last divorce, I was convinced that none of my prayers were really answered. I felt that all the time I had spent pouring over scriptures and praying over my husband and children was for naught because I didn't see any fruit from those prayers. Therefore I decided I would live my life however I saw fit. Oh, I still attended church on a mostly regular basis. I still tithed, and I certainly still believed in God. But I gave up my habits of a morning devotion and prayer time because I was convinced it had not done me a bit of good. Why bother with the do's and don'ts? For at least five years I lived pretty much outside the bounds of my own core beliefs, sleeping with every man I dated and drinking to excess whenever the mood struck. There were no do's and don'ts because I did pretty much whatever I wanted to, whenever I wanted. Over the course of five years I was hurt as a result of my rebellion in pretty much every instance. You could say I was looking for love in all the wrong men, because none of them were what I would consider "my person." I let myself become more deeply involved with each man more than I should have.

The last relationship I was involved in that ended suddenly and without warning left me broken and spent. I believed I was in love with this man. It wasn't the first time I had fallen fast and fallen hard; however, I had opened myself up to him more than I had anyone else since my third divorce. I couldn't understand what had happened at all and probably never will. However, I knew I had to let it go and move forward, and I also knew it was time for a hard reset on my life, to get back to the basics of love... God's love, not the world's view of love. I could hardly wait to get to the beach to commune with the Father because that is where I feel closest to Him. I knew it would take hard work, prayer, and determination to accomplish what I set out to accomplish on that trip... alone with God.

I spent three days on the beach. The first day was spent with clothes on and a blanket wrapped around me because it was pretty chilly in November, but I didn't care. I could feel the peace and love of God there. I took a book with me that focused on inner healing, because I knew my wounds were deep. I walked through the steps of breaking ungodly soul ties with every man I had been involved with so God could restore my soul to wholeness. In the process God revealed to me different areas of my life where I had believed incorrectly. He did this so I could give forgiveness where it was needed, in order to let go and move forward. I did a lot of crying, a lot of praying, a lot of reading, and soaking in the love of God and His grace and mercies. He is a good, good Father and He is so faithful to fulfill his promises. However, He will use our brokenness and heartache to bring us back to Him while He is working everything together for our good and for His most loving outcome. When I arrived on the other side of my weekend at the beach with God, I realized the person who had rejected me was also not "my person" or the husband that God had in mind for me and was able to let go and move on happy and free. God says He will give us the desires of our hearts. I don't believe that means that He will give us "whatever we want" but rather He will place those desires in our hearts. I believe He has given me the desire to be the Godly wife to a Godly husband and He will bring that husband to me. In order to be that Godly wife I had to get back to putting God first in my life, because if not, the Godly husband I desire wouldn't have any interest in me if I met him. In the process I'm learning to enjoy the waiting period because I have a lot to accomplish before he arrives! Besides, anything worth having is worth waiting for. That being said, I can't accomplish anything on my own or of my own strength or power. Without God I have no strength in me, I have no power to do or become anything. In Him, I live and move and have my being.

I am so thankful for a God of loving mercy and kindness who picks me up out of the miry clay in my weakness and failures and comforts and loves me right where I am. I'm thankful I don't have to "clean myself up" to come to the Father and nail everything to the Cross and receive His forgiveness.

There is however, a great deception Satan would have us all believe. I believe one of Satan's greatest deceptions is getting people to believe the lie "what's the big deal anyway?" when God has clearly stated that something is a BIG DEAL. Take Eve for example. The serpent convinced her it would actually be no big deal for her to taste the forbidden fruit in *Genesis 3:4*. In fact he practically laughed at her when she told him God said they would surely die if they ate of the tree of Knowledge…His response was "you will not certainly die." He convinced her God was the one who had deceived them and only wanted them to believe they would die. Satan convinced Eve she was missing out by not eating of the fruit. He convinced her she would be "like God" if she did eat the fruit, that she would know everything God knows. What she failed to realize was she was already "like God" for we are made in His image.

It's the same in life today as it was that day in the Garden of Eden. People are convinced every day by the great deceiver that it is no big deal to "snort that coke," "pop that pill," "tell that lie," "cheat just once," or whatever he may have convinced them would be no big deal to do "just this once." Well guess what? It's all a big deal. Ask the junkie who can't get off drugs. Ask the adulterer whose marriage has been ruined. Ask the friend who has been betrayed by a lie. For the prostitute the lie might be, "what's the big deal if I do it for money? It's not like I'm a virgin anyway." For the habitual, pathological liar, the deception might be, "what's the big deal if I lie? What they don't know won't hurt them."

When we are deceived into believing the things we do which are contrary to the Word of God are "no big deal" we believe the way we see it is "right" but in the end, it is the way of death.

Some more examples of Satan's deception might be: "what's the big deal if I have sex with my significant other; we're planning on getting married someday anyway?" "What's the big deal if I take something that's not mine, I deserve it don't I?" "What's the big deal if I have my children out of wedlock? It's better than getting married just because I'm pregnant and ending up in divorce anyway." "What's the big deal if we just have oral sex? It's not like it's 'real sex' anyway?"

In *John 10:10* the Word of God tells us Satan is a liar and a thief and he has come to lie, steal, kill and destroy God's people. He will seek an "in" wherever he can find one. Whenever we choose to walk in disobedience to God's Word, we are choosing to give Satan the "in" he desperately seeks in order to destroy us. It also says that He (Jesus) came that we might have and enjoy an abundant life.

Jesus died, was crucified, bled and beaten that we might be healed, well, whole, and satisfactorily at peace with God and man. He came that we might have and enjoy abundant life. Are you living the abundant life God has for you? If you're not, is it because you have allowed the great deceiver to blind you to the truth of the Word of God?

Ask yourself right now, "Is there anything I've been thinking of as 'no big deal' when God says that it is a BIG DEAL?" If so, know this, His grace is sufficient for you. His strength is made perfect in your weakness. He's waiting for you to come and commune with Him and nail it all to the Cross. God loves you so much that He sent His only son Jesus Christ to die on a Cross for you. His blood covers every sin you have ever committed, or ever will commit. He paid it all, once and for all. His blood paid your ransom. So if you know you've screwed up, and we all have, fear not, He will never leave you or forsake you. And again, I will say, His grace is sufficient.

While God's grace is always sufficient, if you have received Jesus Christ as your Lord and Savior and you continue to walk, live and conduct yourself in a manner that is contrary to his Word, you are crucifying the Savior over and over again. You're making the blood He shed and the stripes that He bore worthless in your life. I realize that is a harsh reality, but it is reality nonetheless. *James 4:17* says, *"Remember, it is sin to know what you ought to do and then not do it."* Doing what is right is not always the easy thing to do. However, if you have Christ living on the inside, He will give you strength to do all things. 1 Corinthians 10:13 also states, "The temptations in your life are no different from what others experience. And God is faithful. He will not allow the temptation to be more than you can stand. When you are tempted, He will show you a way out so that you can endure." God will make a way when there seems to be no way if we will watch for it and move toward Him.

I often wonder why I personally have continued to do things in my life that I am very well aware are outside the will of God. I was saved at 6 years old and baptized at 7 years old. I believe sex outside of marriage is wrong and definitely a sin. Yet I've participated in that act more times than I care to mention. The only explanation I can give is that I'm human and therefore subject to imperfections just like every other human. The reality is, like everyone in this world, I will not achieve perfection this side of heaven. That doesn't mean we don't try to live right while we are here. It does mean however, that the scripture is very, true *"all have sinned and fallen short of the glory of God."* Even Paul said God gave him a thorn in his flesh to keep him from becoming proud. I feel like my total weakness in the area of "sex outside the boundaries of marriage" has been the "thorn in my flesh" that keeps me from becoming proud or thinking I have achieved anything of my own volition. Again, I can do nothing without my heavenly Father and without the strength of Christ in me. And it seems every time I start thinking more highly of myself than I should, I get brought down several notches by the reality of my very weak flesh. Once again the Greater One in me brings me back to center and reminds me it is only through the strength infused in me through Christ that I can do all things. God's grace is sufficient for me once more.

How would you define grace? Specifically how would you define God's grace? Most Christians would say that it is the unmerited or undeserved favor of God because that's what we have been taught. Fortunately, God gives us what we need, not what we deserve. He also exhibits His great mercy every day by not giving us what we often do deserve.

We cannot earn grace any more than we can earn our way into heaven. Salvation is a free, gift of God. He sent His one and only Son to die on a cross to pay for the gift. We cannot work for it, earn it, or purchase it, because the King of Kings and Lord of Lords already paid the price.

That being said, we should never judge someone else's sin just because it is different than our own. Jesus is the only one who has paid the admission to heaven. We cannot earn our way in or do enough good works. Receiving the salvation that he bought and paid for with the shedding of his blood is the only way. If you could earn your way into Heaven, there would have been no need for Him to suffer and die a humiliating death on a tree. But because He did, we can freely receive God's gift of grace, the gift that "keeps on giving."

Often, we find it difficult to receive the free gift God offers us because we allow our guilt from the things we've done in the past to convince us we are not worthy. The reality is, we are not worthy by our own efforts. Satan enjoys reminding us of our unworthiness by reminding us of our past transgressions. He uses our guilt to shame us into believing we cannot receive the free, gift of grace. He tries to convince us it couldn't possibly be available to us and we couldn't ever be "good enough." He is called the accuser of the brethren in the book of Revelations because he always wants to throw the past into our present.

When we don't seek forgiveness for our sins we open the door for guilt to come in and take root leading to shame and regret. As I noted earlier, we have all sinned and fallen short of the glory of God according to Romans 3:23. If we do not deal appropriately with shame and guilt it will become a foothold for Satan to cause all sorts of problems in our lives. Including all types of illnesses, both physical and mental. For those who refuse to confess their sins the guilt will weigh them down. Sometimes we try to cover over our guilt as our way of dealing with sin. When we do something wrong, we made the choice to do so and if it is not dealt with God's way, it will not get fixed. When you confess your guilt to God, you are then able to obtain his mercy and grace. The reality is, He already knows anyway, so you may as well confess it, lay it before Him and be made free and whole. How long will you allow Satan to make a slave of you because of guilt and shame? When we confess, God cleanses us from ALL unrighteousness. Trust God's character and accept His forgiveness. When you have received the free gift of God's amazing grace, stop doing the thing that caused you shame and guilt in the first place. Walk away from it and do and be different. According to *Philippians 4:13 you can do all things through Christ who gives you strength!*

Chapter 22
Keeping God First in your life...

Matthew 6:33 (AMP) But seek (aim at and strive after) first of all His kingdom and His righteousness (His way of doing and being right), and then all these things taken together will be given you besides.

What do you do to keep God first in your life? Do you seek Him first above all things? Do you seek His kingdom and His righteousness? Is your first desire to know God and have a relationship with Him? He clearly tells us to seek Him first, but He says it with a promise! If we seek Him, all other things will be given to us. That's an awesome thought! God is so good and so BIG and so VAST. He is everything and He owns everything. Every good thing we have is a gift from God. Have you thanked Him for all of your treasures lately? The fact of the matter is this, if you have already received the free gift of salvation that was paid for by the precious blood of His only Son, Jesus Christ, then He has already done enough for. God is so incredibly eat up with and in love with you that He wants to give you all good things. He has a plan just for you. He wants to prosper you. He wants you to be in good health, so if you are sick – yes He wants to heal you. That is His will. Most Christians never live the kind of abundant life God says we can have. But Jesus came so we may have life more abundantly according to *John 10:10 (AMP)* which says, *"The thief comes only in order to steal and kill and destroy. I came that they may have and enjoy life, and have it in abundance (to the full, till it overflows)."*

Our words cannot begin to describe adequately everything that God is or can or wants to be for us. He will be our everything if we will allow Him to do so. It doesn't matter what our problem or need is, Jesus is and always will be the answer. He is our Comforter, our Healer, our Friend who is always with us, our Strong Deliverer, our Provider, our Guide in all things. How can we not keep Him first in our lives or seek Him first thing every morning? We have no breath of life without Him.

You have to let God be your everything including your Peace of Mind in times of trouble and stressful situations. He will be your everything if you will let Him.

Do you struggle with trying to keep God first in your life? Or do you have pre-set uncompromising boundaries? If your children see you compromise your Christianity by not keeping God first in your life, then they too will become "compromising Christians."

I encourage you to find a church home to celebrate God with others and "do life" with your brothers and sisters in Christ. God tells us not to forsake the fellowship of others as some are in the habit of doing. That means once you find a church home you also go to that church when there are services being held. You don't stay home in bed on Sunday morning just because you don't "feel" like getting up because you stayed up too late the night before. The flesh and the spirit man will war with each other until the end of the world as we know it.

Satan desires to steal our joy and our spiritual productivity. If you honor the Lord, He will honor you, because we reap what we sow.

Our lives are a reflection of what's going on inside of us. If Jesus Christ is the Lord of your life then you're going to let Him tell you how to live it. You have to study the Bible to develop your faith. When people fail to seek the kingdom of God and His righteousness first, they do not accomplish what He desires for them. We need the Word of God to solve our problems. Every person was created for a reason and a divine purpose from God and there is nothing God can't do through us if we will learn to obey Him.

One man changed the world with His sacrifice. He was always asking people to do that which was impossible for them to do, without Him. If you obey the Word of God, it can give you the ability to do things you would not normally be able to do on your own. We should always rely on God's promises in His word over what we may be feeling.

Satan doesn't have to get you to go out into the world and sin. He just has to distract you a bit and get your focus on something else besides God. Are you easily distracted? Or do you have a one track mind that's headed straight for Jesus Christ?

Oftentimes people cannot keep God as the center of their lives because they've made something else the center. It may be another person – wife, husband, children, parents, friends, or it may be a job, hobby, or habit. The fact is, anything you put before God is an idol to you and you can't possibly seek God first.

We have to be able to step back and see the big picture because nothing we do in this life matters if it does not have eternal value for the kingdom. If we will focus ourselves on the will of God and His purpose and plan for our lives, He will give us everything else that we're trying to get anyway. When we get our focus right, then we can move into a spirit of joy. We can either be ever reaching for the blessing, or we can embrace the One who gives the blessings. As for me, I choose to embrace the One who blesses, for where would I be without His awesome grace?

I would encourage you to press into the presence of God daily. There is absolutely no better place to be...and oh how awesome it is to be in relationship with the almighty God who created you.

Chapter 23
Surrender

Our life here on this earth is not actually about us, it is about God and what He wants to accomplish through us for others. He gave His one and only son to die on a cross so He could have our hearts. He wants us to surrender all that we have, all that we are, all our hopes, dreams, and everything we ever hope to be to him, so He can help us reach our full potential. Before anyone ever had an opinion of us, God had a purpose for us.

Obedience to God will always require sacrifice on our part. We will always have to give up something to pursue Him. We are called to walk by faith and not by sight. So, when you are walking by faith you don't have to know how God will work in a situation, you just have to know that He is working.

Acts 17:27-28 (NLT)
[27] "His purpose was for the nations to seek after God and perhaps feel their way toward him and

find him—though he is not far from any one of us. *28 For in him we live and move and exist.*

Without God we are nothing, can do nothing, and can be nothing. In Him we live and move and have our being. So, it is through Him that all things are done. However, because He created us with free will, it is up to us to surrender our will to Him so He can accomplish His perfect plan and purpose in our lives.

I have certain ideas and thoughts about what I want for my life. God says He will give me the desires of my heart. But that doesn't mean He will give me whatever I want; rather, He will implant His desires into my heart. I have to surrender my will to Him daily, especially when I don't see in the natural the things I have been praying, come to fruition. I'm reminded of many scriptures when I want things to go a certain way. I stop then and say, nevertheless Lord, not my will, but Your will be done in my life.

Psalm 55:22 (NLT)

Give your burdens to the Lord, and he will take care of you. He will not permit the godly to slip and fall.

Giving our burdens to the Lord is yet another form of surrender. Isn't it wonderful that when we give our burdens to Him, He will not permit us to slip and fall? If you will submit yourself to God and surrender all that you are to Him, He will release his power to accomplish His purpose. You can have what God wants you to have, but you have to pursue Him to get it.

Anything worth having is worth waiting for. In the "waiting" is some of the hardest seasons to walk through. We live in a microwave society where we are not taught to wait on anything. Then we get discouraged when we are waiting on God to do something and we begin to worry and wonder whether He will be faithful to fulfill His promises. God's timing is not our timing and His ways are not our ways. Wait on whatever it is God has placed in your heart. Don't try to take things into your own hands, but rather surrender them to Him. We can't take God and mold Him into our plans, we must allow Him to mold us into His plan.

Salvation

Ephesians 2:8-9 (NIV)
[8] For it is by grace you have been saved, through faith—and this is not from yourselves, it is the gift of God— [9] not by works, so that no one can boast.

As we see in these verses it is by grace and through faith that we are saved from our sins and it is a gift of God. We cannot do anything to earn salvation. If you have never given your life to Christ, and asked Him to come into your heart and be the Lord of your life, I invite you to do so now. It is my passion to share His love and grace and for others to know what He has done for me, He can and will do for you. All you have to do is ask.

Father, please forgive me of all my sins. Create in me a clean and pure heart that longs to follow hard after You. By faith I invite You to come live in my heart right now and be the Lord of my life. Thank You for all that You have done for me. In Jesus' precious name I pray, amen.

Made in the USA
Monee, IL
09 July 2020